SCHIRMER'S LIBRARY
OF MUSICAL CLASSICS

Vol. 1405

Camille Saint-Saëns

Second Concerto
In G minor

For Piano and Orchestra

The orchestral score
Arranged for a Second Piano

Op. 22

Edited by

ISIDOR PHILIPP

ISBN 978-0-7935-3887-4

G. SCHIRMER, Inc.

DISTRIBUTED BY

HAL•LEONARD®
CORPORATION

7777 W. BLUEMOUND RD. P.O. BOX 13819 MILWAUKEE, WI 53213

A Mme. A. de Villers née de Huber

Second Concerto

Edited by
Isidor Philipp

I

C. Saint-Saëns, Op. 22

Piano I
(Solo)

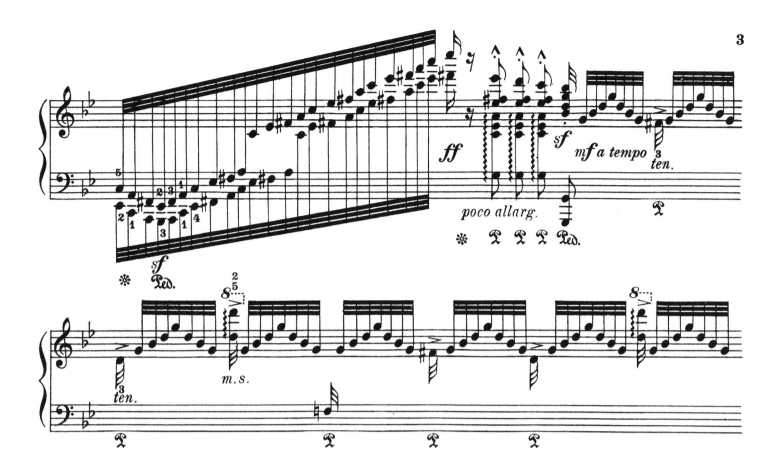

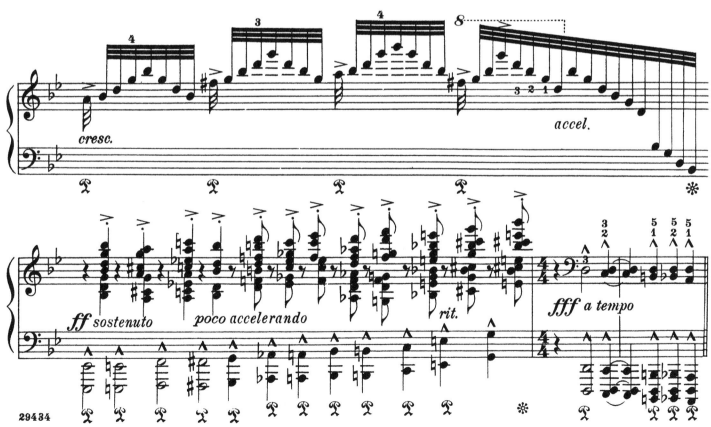

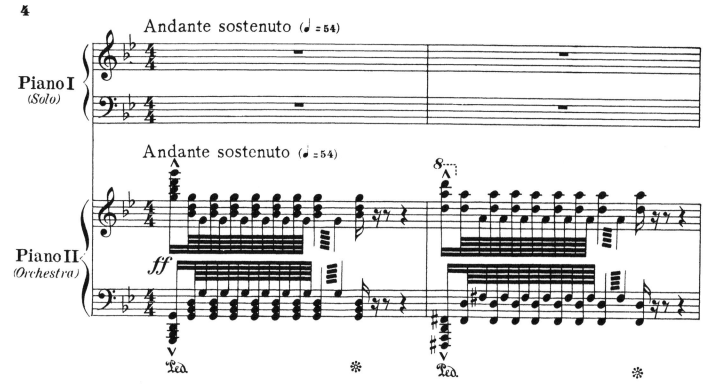

Sempre più animato

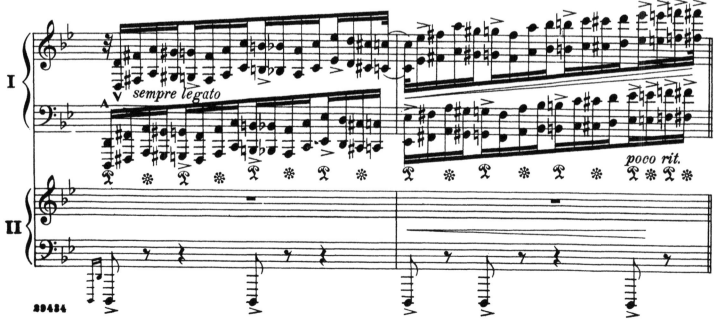

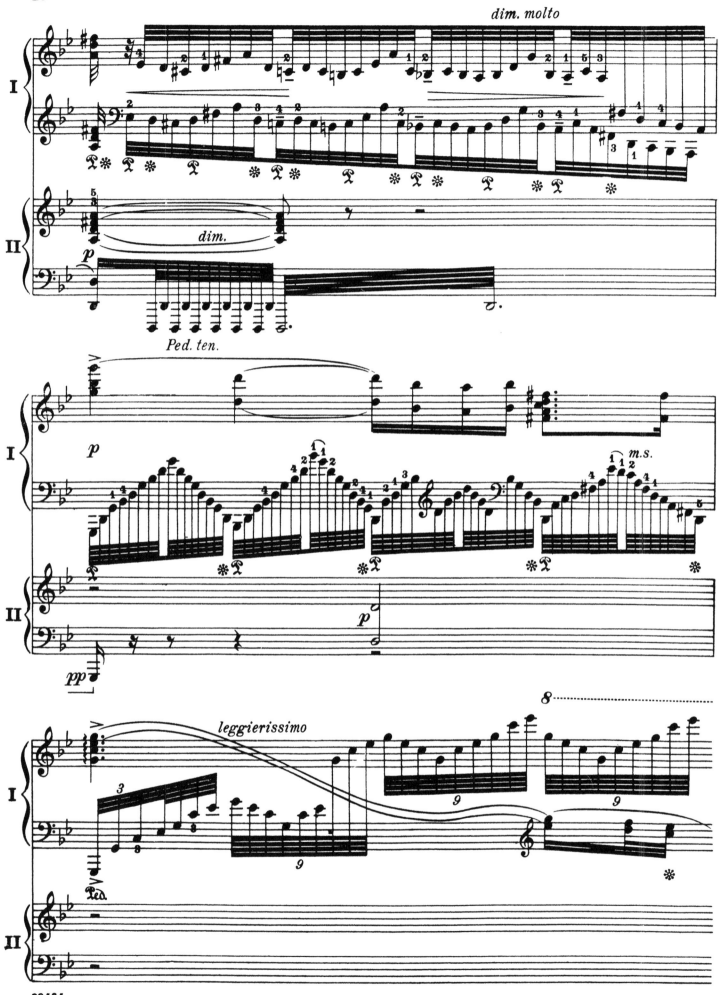

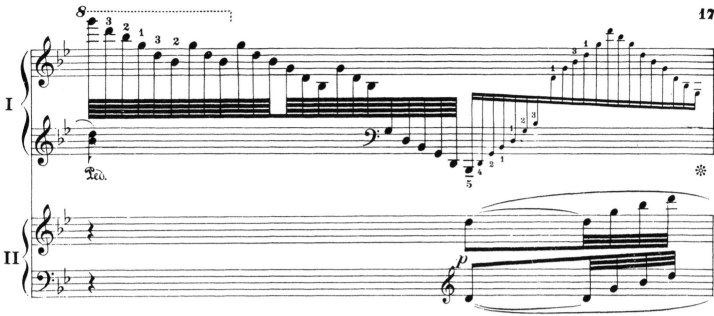

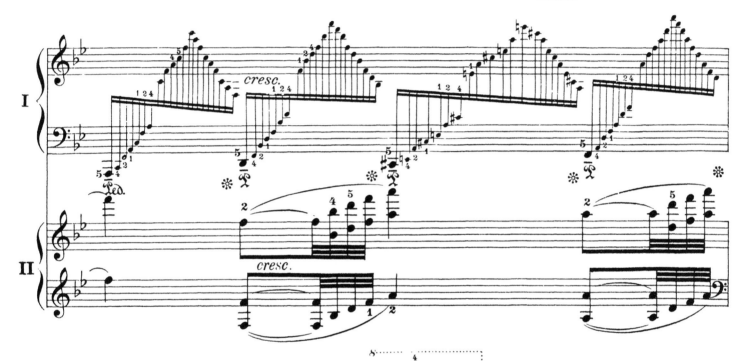

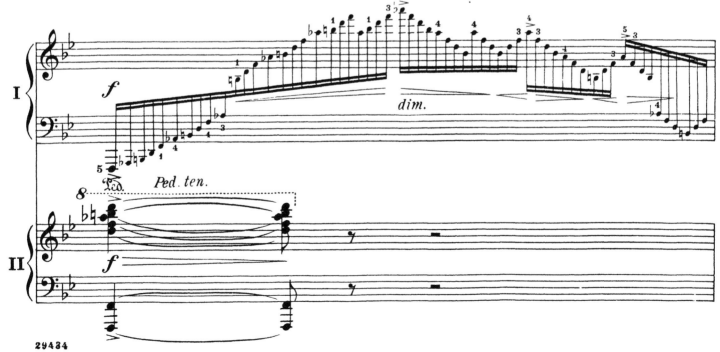

29434

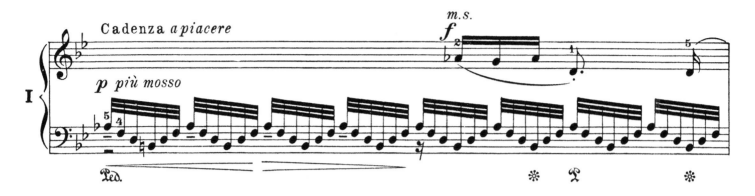

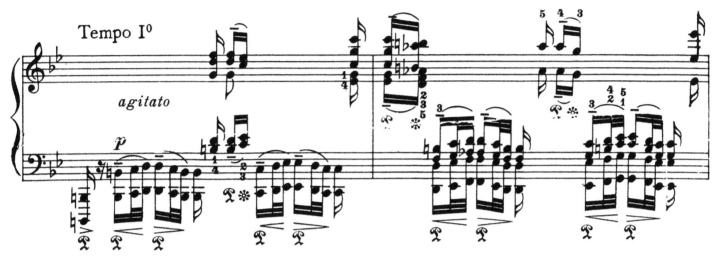

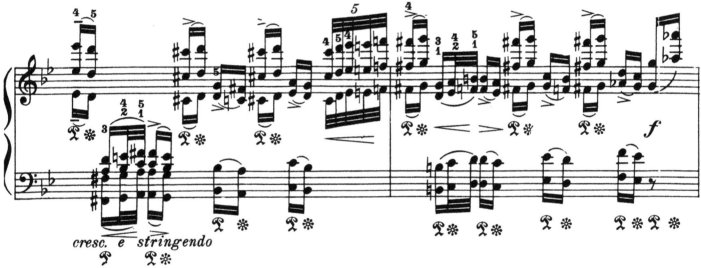

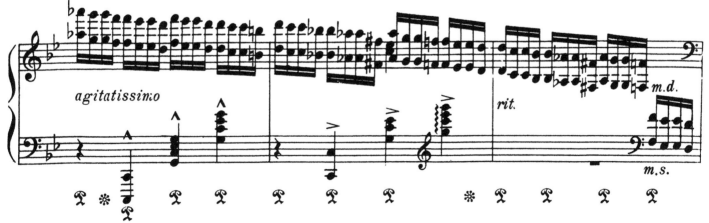

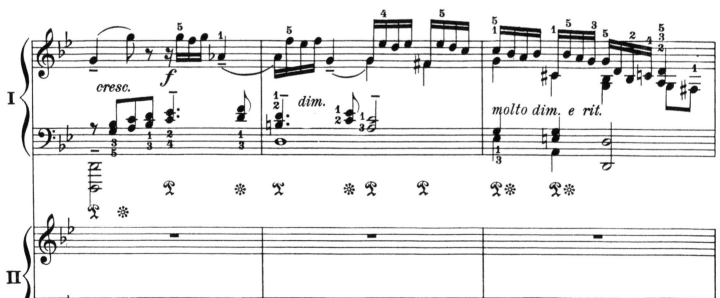

II

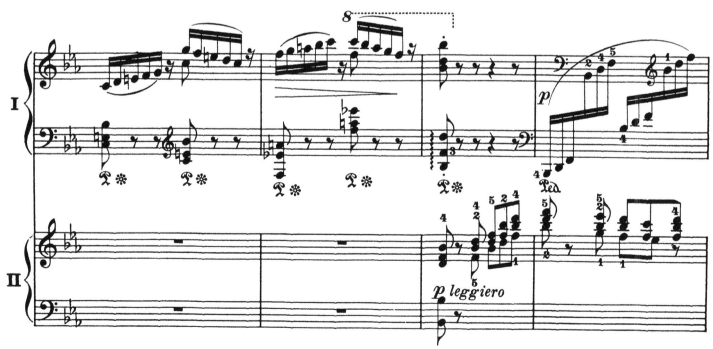

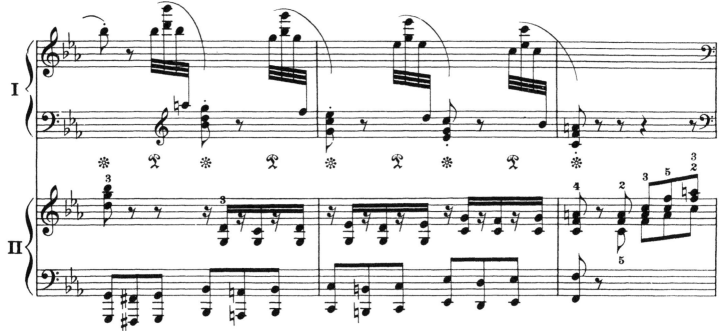

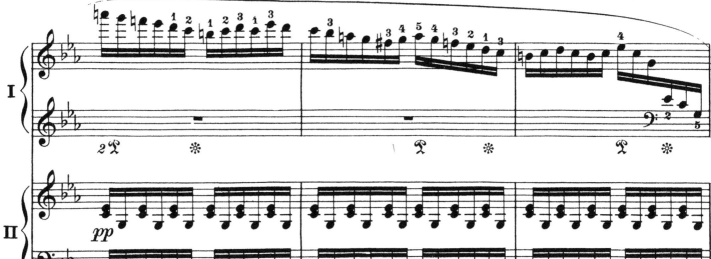

29434

29484

29484

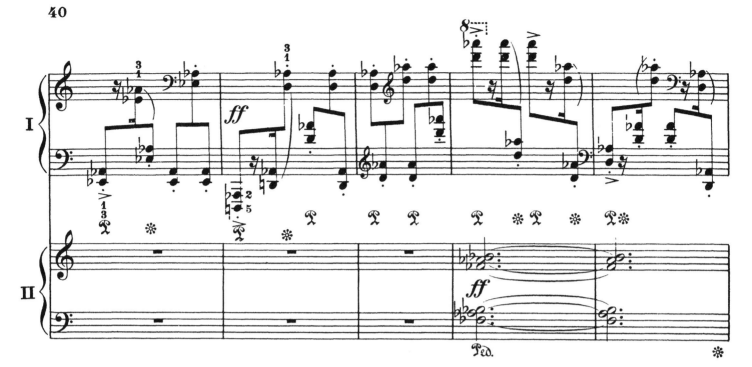

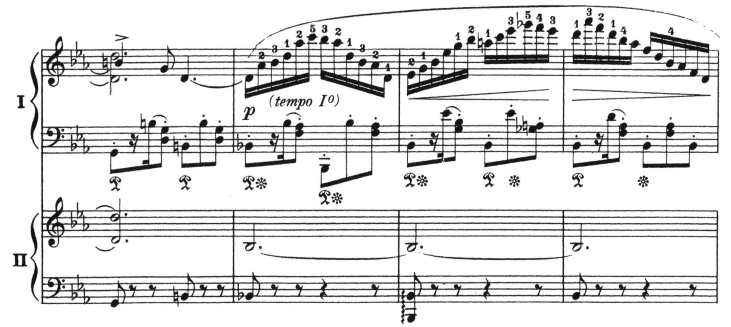

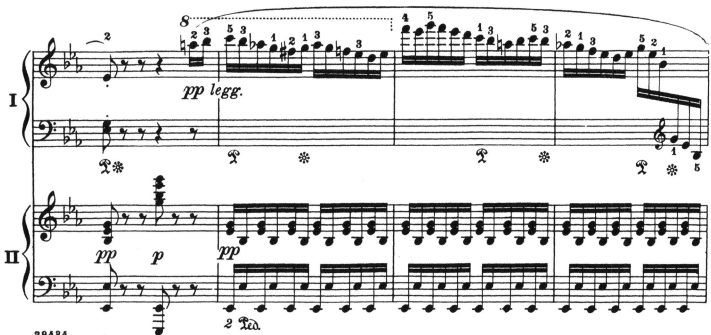

29484

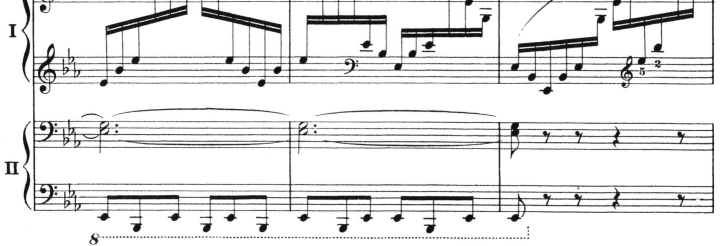

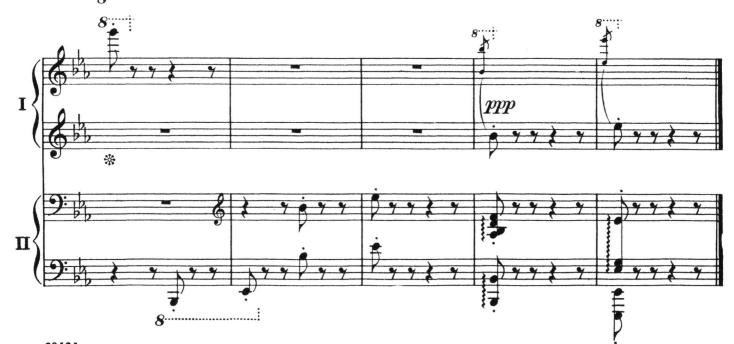

III

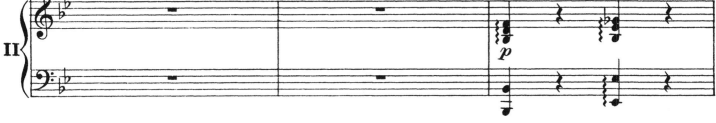

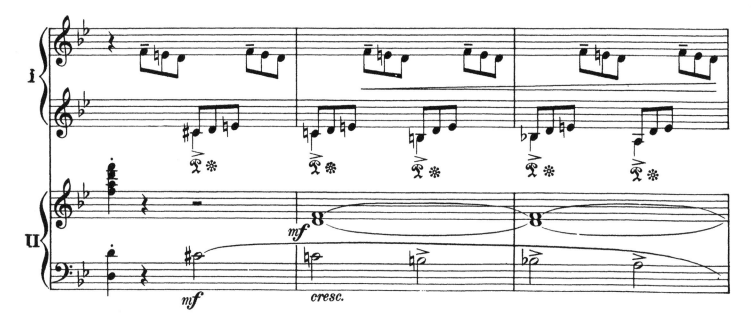

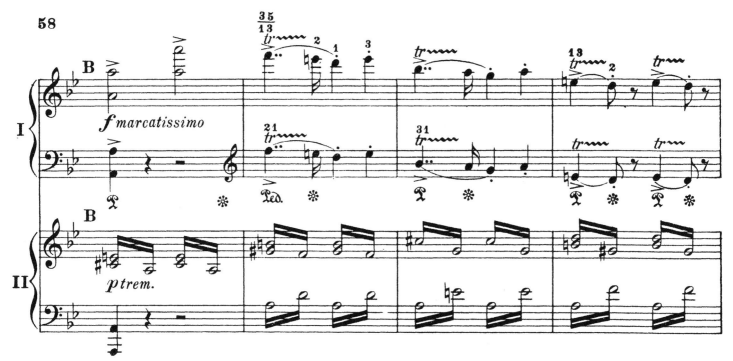

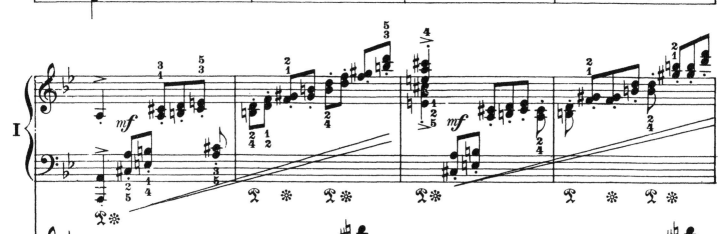

29434

poco a poco crescendo

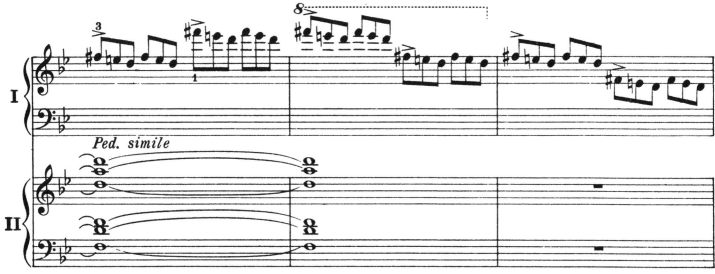

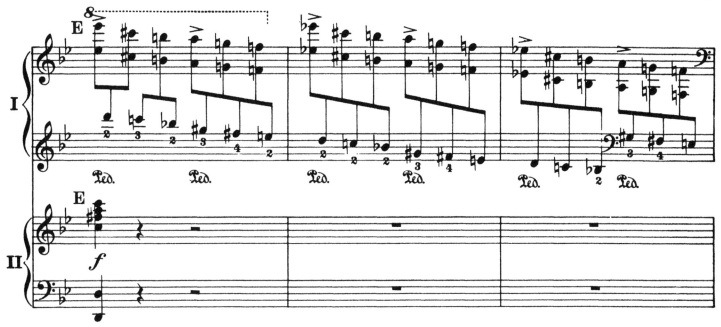

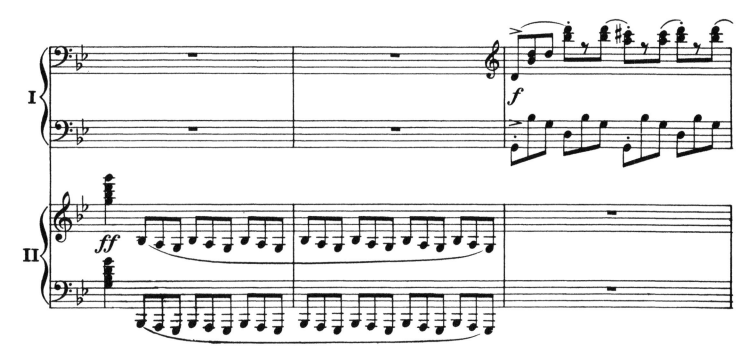

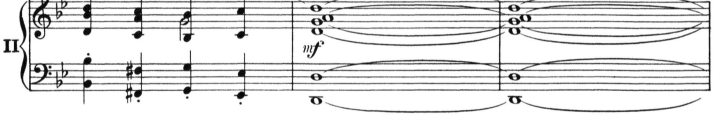

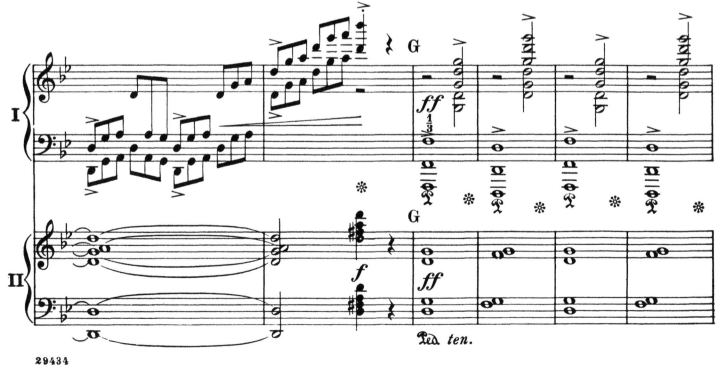

29434